Seeking Spirits:
A Sensitive's Journey

Shining Crow Books
2-1 Oxford Street
Cambridge, Ontario N1R 1M1, Canada

Copyright ©2016, Sheila J. Watson
All rights reserved.

ISBN: 978-0-9952836-1-9
Copyright information available upon request.

Cover Design: Mark Saloff Designs
Cover Image Adapted from: ©iStockPhoto.com/Robertiez
Interior Art: © iStockPhoto.com/Epine Art and Vera Petruk
Interior Design: J. L. Saloff
Typography: Perpetua

All rights reserved. Printed in the United States of America. No part of this book may be used or reproduced in any manner whatsoever without written permission except in the case of brief quotations embodied in critical articles and reviews.

The scanning, uploading and distribution of this book via the Internet or via any other means without permission of the publisher is illegal and punishable by law. Please purchase only authorized electronic editions, and do not participate in or encourage electronic piracy of copyrighted materials. Your support of the author's rights is appreciated.

v. 1.0
First Edition, 2016
Printed on acid free paper.

Scripture taken from the NEW AMERICAN STANDARD BIBLE®, Copyright © 1960,1962,1963,1968,1971,1972,1973,1975,1977, 1995 by The Lockman Foundation. Used by permission.

With much love to Janna, Jason, Christopher and Victoria,

To Grandma Daisy and her brother, Uncle Bobby,

And to my many teachers, both in the spirit world and on the earth plane, for knowledge is the greatest gift of all.

ACKNOWLEDGMENTS

I would like to acknowledge my wonderfully talented and supportive editors, Jamie Saloff and Pat Matson. I could not have done it without you.

DISCLAIMER

Some names and details have been changed to protect the privacy of the individuals involved.

Seeking Spirits:
A Sensitive's Journey

How I Learned to Work With the Spirit World

Rev. Sheila J. Watson

Shining Crow Books

Contents

Preface: Are You a Seeker? 1

Chapter One: Being Sensitive 5

Chapter Two: Mysticism 17

Chapter Three: Dealing With Religious Doctrines 25

Chapter Four: Psychic Development 31

Chapter Five: Truth, Mediumship and
    Spiritual Development 59

Chapter Six: Advanced Forms of Mediumship 77

Chapter Seven: Healing 91

Chapter Eight: Growth and Enlightenment 99

Chapter Nine: Call to Action 107

Resources 111

Bibliography & References 113

Suggested Reading 117

Endnotes 119

Preface

ARE YOU A SEEKER?

I was the product of a broken home, my parents having split when I was only three-and-a-half years old. My mother and I moved in with Mom's parents, and Grandma Daisy raised me. I grew up without brothers or sisters. I had a lot of time to play by myself in our big yard with trees and high hedges all around it. I was not allowed to leave the property by myself, and very few playmates passed my Grandma's high standards.

It could have been a very boring childhood, except I had a huge internal life. My mind was chasing ideas all the time.

"Grandma, if God made everything, who made God?"

SEEKING SPIRITS

When she said she did not have the answer, I sat in the back yard and talked to God myself. "Who made you, God? I don't understand. How could you make yourself?" I listened quietly for an answer. It did feel like there was someone there with me. I was sure of it.

Grandma told me if I wanted answers I should read the Bible. My reading skills were about the same as any other eight-year-old girl, but I sat down with her each day and read a chapter to her from the King James Bible. No doubt it improved my reading, but I did not understand much more about God than before.

I got angry when I did not understand, and veered between proclaiming myself an atheist like my Uncle Bobby, and asking to go to church by myself because my family did not go to church at all.

Yes, Uncle Bobby the atheist, and Grandpa, the lapsed Methodist who criticized church hypocrisy in loud family discussions, were great examples to me. So was Grandma who was highly-gifted both intellectually and spiritually, and could hold her own in any discussion. They were examples of how to be a spiritual rebel — in fact, a seeker.

You see, a seeker does not accept what

Preface

they are told. They want to understand for themselves. If they find they are on a spiritual path that is only an illusion, they will seek elsewhere.

So are you a seeker?

Chapter One

BEING SENSITIVE

Each night, I catch a Red Rocket streetcar eastbound at College Park. I sit back and watch the world go by — literally the world.

We travel Carlton Street, past the bars, the shops, the excited and eccentric Torontonians of every description. I watch them and enjoy their energy.

Next appears Allan Gardens with its poor who sit in the park or get on the streetcar with their small bundles of worldly possessions. I feel sad and yet I know some of them are happier than some of the very rich. I say nothing.

Cabbagetown Women's Clinic comes next, where

women in crisis exercise their Freedom of Choice. A burly guard in a yellow jacket protects the door. Every day across the street, protestors hold pictures of pretty little babies in pink or blue blankets, and pictures of fetuses and embryos. They exercise their Freedom of Voice. Again feeling sad, I say nothing.

But the stop after that cheers me up a bit. The Gerrard Street Projects are low-cost housing for the poor and new immigrants. It is a make-or-break community that has spawned great successes as well as many failures. In the morning, I sometimes see women in black burkas walking their children to school. Yes, the whole world is right here on the way home — just everyone.

A young, bearded man gets on the streetcar with his two-year-old boy riding on his shoulders. The boy acts excited and wants to stay with the driver. Everyone smiles. The driver toots his horn to the rhythm, "Shave and a haircut, two bits." The child giggles.

Chinatown's hustle and bustle arrives after that with merchandise piled outside in front of their shops. Everyone scurries about in a great hurry.

Then Degrassi Street! The driver calls out "Eastdale Collegiate," where the Degrassi TV show was originally filmed. I somehow feel we are traveling through history.

Being Sensitive

And now Riverdale appears with its quiet desperate people looking for a leg up and there stands the Anglican church with its suppers for the poor. Then Leslieville, with homes that seem steeped in history.

Oh, my stop is coming up soon...yes, Little India with the aromas of its exotic spices. I get out by the Tikka House, walk to a side street, then turn down an alley. Beside my dwelling, a young Indian couple sits on the steps sharing Indian take out. We exchange greetings. "It's always nice to show friendliness to the neighbors," I figure.

Ah, and then I'm home. I'm in the door to my peaceful, quiet flat. The cat greets then cuddles me. So much for the world tour. I'm putting my feet up. I breathe in deeply. There is no noise whatsoever. If I listen, I can hear the sound of my heartbeat while I think back on the day. Now this is home! I can replenish my energies.

Toronto is not too busy after all. I don't have to flee or move far away. As long as I have a simple sanctuary, a place of peace, I always have a home. Going home is as much about a state of mind as it is reaching a physical destination.

I wrote those words in 2010. It was a pleasure to tell my friends about my evening journey home. The sensory richness of the trip helped me get my mind off work. I embraced the circumstances in which I lived and shared them with others so they might understand me better. Yet, I was not being entirely truthful.

The fact is, I am an extremely sensitive, naturally-psychic person. I was never okay in the emotional roughness of the big city. I could feel the emotions of other people, and there were so many other people. I always knew when someone held me in contempt. I was hurting a lot of the time. Working in a big company was hard, too. I did not belong in the bump-and-grind in which I lived, and I could not – would not – mold myself into a different person.

I have a natural sensitivity so it's no wonder I feel uncomfortable around some people. I could read what they were really like. No wonder I liked some other people automatically. I knew they were good. No wonder I was so unhappy at work. The people I worked with had completely different values and did not care for anyone who would not or could not conform.

Our society teaches us what is possible and what is not. Spend some time watching a young child with an imaginary playmate. There is a possibility that they are not imagining at all. They are talking to a spirit. By the time that child reaches kindergarten age, they learn to ignore such a spirit playmate.

Being Sensitive

Their parents may even have accused them of lying. Certainly, other children may ridicule them. They forget their spiritual gifts and conform to what society teaches.

We learn that it is impossible to read others. If we get impressions, we put them to the back of our mind and may even wonder about our own mental health. The fact is, the gift of being psychic was there all along. Perhaps it is for you, as well. Are you curious yet? Have you had these experiences?

What if I told you it is possible for an adult of any age to rediscover their natural childhood abilities? What if I told you that it is possible to develop your natural psychic gift to an expert level? What if you learned that spiritual development will make you a better and happier person? The truth is, no one becomes a psychic. The gift was always there. Remember Dorothy in the Wizard of Oz? "You had the power all along."

Too Fast A Pace

Being me felt all just too much. This was not the world I grew up in with my grandparents. The pace had never been faster. No one should live like this, especially those of us with strong psychic gifts. Something had to change. And yet, the 21st century is an extraordinary time to live on Earth.

We Baby Boomers have lived long enough to see changes our parents and grandparents would struggle to grasp. I grew up on the outskirts of a small Ontario city in the 1950s. I remember old-fashioned milk delivery trucks, ice boxes, and outhouses. My cousins pumped water from their own well. Our family was not unusual for those times.

There was one telephone company, and we thought the technology was marvelous! Telephones came in your choice of black or black. They had rotary dials, and we shared the party line with one or more of our neighbors. If you picked up the line, you might hear Mrs. Smith discussing the state of her digestion with the local pharmacist. Neighborhood feuds sometimes developed over telephone eavesdropping. The line was a community resource.

Since that time, the speed of technology-induced change is almost unfathomable. Our world continuously moves faster and is becoming increasingly one global – if discordant – community. Modern technology is everywhere. We are constantly engaged with other people's ideas and encouraged to conform, which may include spending beyond our means for the latest toys. It is difficult to break free from an unwise financial pattern.

Yet human beings have not changed very much at all. I can state from first-hand experience and observation that no matter how brilliant, wealthy, or accomplished a person is, that alone is not enough to bring inner peace. Humanity still has the same spiritual needs it had thousands of years ago. The still small voice from within can always be found. I have discovered that when that urge pulls me from within, I must seek to make it manifest in the world around me. You may have felt this urge, too.

My Search Begins

I felt a bit lonely in my Toronto apartment one Saturday night in the summer of 2006. I went across the street and caught a subway train, then a streetcar to a somewhat dilapidated — yet enticing — old building in the Portuguese part of town. It was a former Christian Church converted to a more eclectic worship center. It was a Christian Spiritualist church. I had never been in such an exotic place.

There was a Message Service that night. I sat in the very back row with my back to the wall. I was wearing dark clothing and being as unobtrusive as possible.

They started with some old-fashioned hymns, then spiritual healing, a short sermon, collection, and announcements. Indeed, it seemed like most any other church anywhere. Then the message portion of the service began.

Reverend Gordon paced back and forth on the platform at the front of the church. It seemed odd to me, but I would later learn he was just raising energy to work better. He would call out to one person at a time in the congregation of perhaps a hundred people. Then he would give them each an inspirational message. It was either a word of encouragement or a message from one of their deceased loved ones. This went on for perhaps twenty minutes. Then it happened.

"You," Reverend Gordon called out. "You in the back row. Put up your hand. Yes, you!"

Shyly I raised my hand.

"You're a minister! Has anyone told you that? You should study at some place. You can study here if you want to!"

This was rather bold of Reverend Gordon, as his home church was not in Toronto at all, but Ottawa. He was only a visitor.

I was very surprised and I wondered if such people ever make mistakes. What had made me go there that night? It felt as if I was really supposed to go there — as if it was the *only* place I should experience that Saturday night. I would continue to ponder this issue. It felt so right there, so good. I felt as if I belonged somehow. I was not a person who often felt a sense of belonging, so I knew that something special had happened, and I held it in my heart.

Being Sensitive

Following My Path

It would be some time, and several churches later before I felt comfortable enough to study, but study is what I did. I am forever a student of the Spirit world. The still small voice continues to bring me forward.

My curiosity was leading me. I searched around for teachers to help me find a spiritual truth that made sense to me. I wanted to understand life and had become frustrated with traditional religions. If psychic ability is true, and I sensed it was, then a true spiritual path will address it as well as other relevant life issues. Is this not perfectly logical?

You will see me quote from Holy Scripture. This is because the truths of Christian wisdom literature are deeply engrained within me, and form my communication of inspiration. I also have a fondness for wisdom literature from other faiths.

I am not trying to convert you to Christianity, Spiritualism, or anything else. You deserve better than that. You are a free spirit and can find your own truth when it is time.

It seems my motto in life has been, "Why do anything the easy way when you can do it the hard way?" I really have done a survey of a variety of religions and paths. I was not always sure what I was seeking, but a quiet inner voice said,

"Keep looking." I had a spiritual thirst not easily quenched.

After I started researching Spiritualist churches in Toronto, I eventually found myself attending a small, storefront church where, frankly, there were sometimes more ordained Spiritualist ministers in attendance than congregants. The ordained ministers had received their ordination from various churches at various times. I did not feel an affinity with any of them.

Then I met Barbara. Barbara was different. Something in her energy felt familiar to my soul. "Whoever ordained her," my inner voice said, "is the person who should ordain me."

Barbara gave me information about Lily Dale, New York and *The School of Spiritual Healing and Prophecy*, otherwise known as *Fellowships of the Spirit*. It would become my church home, and I became ordained there in May 2009. The basis of our spiritual program was highly mystical. I learned and progressed in a whole new way.

I believe the Spirit world, the world eternal, is the best part of life. The one true asset is the kingdom of heaven, called in the Bible *the pearl of great price*[1]. (Matthew 13:45-46, NASB)

There are many ways to begin to approach the spiritual kingdom, including prayer, meditation, and service. "But seek first His kingdom and His righteousness, and all these things will be added to you." (Matthew 6:33, NASB) *These things* means the things you need, not necessarily everything that you think you want. You will find a way if it is the path to which you are called. If it is, you will not find happiness with anything less.

If you are highly psychic, service to Spirit may include using these gifts, perhaps professionally.

Chapter Two

MYSTICISM

Mysticism encompasses many ideas, both modern and ancient. Here is its definition:

1. "Belief that union with or absorption into the Deity or the absolute, or the spiritual apprehension of knowledge inaccessible to the intellect, may be attained through contemplation and self-surrender. For example, St. Theresa's writings were part of traditional Christian mysticism,

2. Vague or ill-defined religious or spiritual belief, especially as associated with a belief in the occult."[2]

Seeking Spirits

Mysticism respects religion, yet pushes past dogma to embrace God and Spirit with love. It is the very essence of true religion and brings meaning to our doctrines and liturgy. Mysticism is, in fact, our love affair with the Universe. Mysticism is not a New Age phenomenon. It is as old as humanity.

The religions of the world, as diverse as they are, provide comforting environments for those who need them. They are like warm, fuzzy, protective blankets for those in despair. Beliefs become doctrines, and doctrines become rules and regulations. Some people prefer this security and will never look further. That is their path. You may have grown up on that path, but is it still yours?

If you are a true seeker, you will not find contentment with the path or the words of others. You will want your own journey. This is the way of the Mystic.

You may take comfort in the knowledge that you are not the first on such a path. Mysticism has its foundations within the realms of religion over millennia. Let's look briefly at a few forms of Mysticism practised today. Even if you do not embrace any of the larger belief systems, they will give you some context.

Mysticism

Christian Mysticism

The term mysticism is a Greek word meaning *to conceal*.[3] Mysticism referred to the spiritual and contemplative side of early and medieval Christianity.[4] Mystics came from many religious orders and included such people as St. Hildegard of Bingen, St. Bernard of Clairvaux, and St. Francis of Assisi. They also came from a variety of geographic locations such as Meister Eckhart from Germany, and Teresa of Avila from Spain.

After the reformation, the writings of lay visionaries such as Emanuel Swedenborg and William Blake were developed, as well as the foundation of mystical movements like the Quakers. Catholic mysticism continued with such figures as Padre Pio and Thomas Merton.

Jewish Mysticism

In modern times, Judaism has had two main kinds of mysticism: Merkabah mysticism and Kabbalah. The former predated the latter, and focused on visions such as those mentioned in the Book of Ezekiel. Merkabah is the Hebrew word meaning chariot, a reference to Ezekiel's vision of a fiery chariot composed of heavenly beings.[5]

Kabbalah is a set of esoteric teachings meant to explain

the relationship between an unchanging eternity and the created universe. In the 20th and 21st centuries, interest in Kabbalah from both Jewish and non-Jewish seekers has flourished.[6]

Islamic Mysticism

According to scholars, Sufism is a science to help the heart focus only on God. Sufi practitioners are dervishes. Their religious orders are not closed like Christian monastic orders. The members retain an outside life.[7]

Buddhism

The main aim of Buddhism is liberation from the cycle of rebirth by enlarging self-awareness and self-control.[8] The Buddhist tradition rejects the notion of a permanent self.

Hinduism

Hinduism has a number of interlinked traditions and schools which aim at moksha[9] (emancipation, liberation or release) and the acquisition of higher powers.[10]

Theosophy

Theosophy – *God's wisdom* in Greek – refers to systems of thought about the mysteries of life, such as divinity.

Mysticism

Theosophy is a part of esotericism, which refers to various studies regarding the mysteries of the universe.

In 1875, the Theosophical Society originated in New York City with the motto, "There is no Religion higher than Truth."[11] There were originally six founders, including Emma Hardinge Britten, one of the pioneers of modern Spiritualism. Due to a falling out, the founders became Helena Petrovna Blavatsky, Henry Steel Olcott, and William Quan Judge.

The declared objectives of Theosophy were:

> *1. To form a nucleus of the universal brotherhood of humanity, without distinction of race, creed, sex, caste or color,*
>
> *2. To encourage the study of comparative religion, philosophy and science,*
>
> *3. To investigate the unexplained laws of Nature and the powers latent in man.*[12]

In the 1920s, the Theosophical Society had around 7,000 members in the United States.[13] Through history, the Theosophists influenced the Indian Independence movement and Buddhist and Hindu reform movements.[14]

Seeking Spirits

New Age Movement

Our present-day New Age Movement is largely based on original Theosophical ideas. "No single organization or movement has contributed so many components to the New Age Movement as the Theosophical Society. It has been the major force to distribute occult literature in the West in the twentieth century."[15]

The above is a simple overview of some of the mystical traditions. There are far too many to list all of them here. These traditions endure because they fill a spiritual need.

Why Do We Bother?

I believe we bother to take this journey, which I refer to as my mad little path of spiritual adventure, because intuitively we are looking for the meaning of life. We are not sure it is simply referenced and outlined in any of the holy books. Yes, they are a start, and many people will look no further. And yet…the heart knows…the psyche is aware…your intuitive abilities are twitching. There is more! You know there is more! The religious organizations do not generally allude much to mysticism. Perhaps that is because it is your own path. Once you are on the path of independent seeking, they cannot control you. You are free to explore.

Mysticism

The Meaning Of Life!

Ah yes, the meaning of life. Surely a spiritual path should get there eventually. Do you really think it is about rules, regulations and punishment? My personal view is it all comes together around love. God is love, and love is all there is. However, you must decide that for yourself.

Chapter Three

DEALING WITH RELIGIOUS DOCTRINES

I consider myself blessed being raised in a family with very mixed opinions about religion. I was given different viewpoints from an early age and encouraged to think for myself. I veered in every direction, including mainstream Christianity. Eventually, I found Spiritualism but I am still learning and growing and incorporate other influences. I feel free to do so.

Not everyone is so fortunate. Some people grow up in strict, religious homes – generally Christian – where doctrine and dogma govern much of day-to-day living. When these folks reach adulthood, they often find it difficult to question their ingrained beliefs. They feel guilty if they do not follow the dogma of their childhood.

You may have experienced this yourself. If you have followed me this far, you have likely worked out most of these emotions, yet you may have family members and friends who do not understand the ideas you are exploring. They may even be worried about you.

Probably you just want a way to reassure them so they will leave you in peace. You do not want a lengthy discussion. If you are hoping to get your family interested in your path, remember they will only become curious when they are ready spiritually and psychologically. Not everyone will be ready in this lifetime.

It is good to go back to the source, the religious text, to address deep concerns. For Christians, try this Scripture:

"Teacher, which is the great commandment in the Law?" And He said to him, "'You shall love the Lord your God with all your heart, and with all your soul, and with all your mind.' This is the great and foremost commandment. The second is like it, 'You shall love your neighbor as yourself.' On these two commandments depend the whole Law and the Prophets." (Matthew 22:36-40, NASB)

This is such a powerful Scripture. It tells us love is more important than the code of the law. It speaks to anyone who considers the New Testament a holy book. As long as we are acting in love, trying to help others with our work, we

Dealing With Religious Doctrines

are following in the footsteps of Jesus and we are honoring God.

Additionally, if you are developing your own intuitive practices, your loved ones may still be worried if such gifts are okay with God. Let's look at the following Scripture:

"Truly, truly, I say to you, he who believes in Me, the works that I do, he will do also; and greater works than these he will do; because I go to the Father." (John 14:12, NASB)

In other words, Jesus has said we are following in his footsteps when we perform the miracles he did. He received inspiration direct from the spiritual realm, whether you call that God, angels, guides, or other wise ones. He performed amazing healings. Many of us will be spiritual healers of various types. We will talk about healing later.

What sort of miracles are these? Does God really mean for us to perform these? Here is an answer:

> *"Now there are varieties of gifts, but the same Spirit. And there are varieties of ministries, and the same Lord. There are varieties of effects, but the same God who works all things in all persons. But to each one is given the manifestation of the Spirit for the common good. For to one is given the <u>word of wisdom</u> through the Spirit, and to another the <u>word of knowledge</u> according to the same Spirit; to another*

faith by the same Spirit, and to another <u>gifts of healing</u> by the one Spirit, and to another the <u>effecting of miracles</u>, and to another <u>prophecy</u>, and to another the <u>distinguishing of spirits</u>, to another <u>various kinds of tongues</u>, and to another the <u>interpretation of tongues</u>. But one and the same Spirit works all these things, distributing to each one individually just as He wills." (1 Corinthians 12:4-11, NASB) (Emphasis added.)

Finally, there are those people who will quote Scripture and talk about evil spirits being involved in any spiritual work that does not agree with their religious path. I really hope you do not have to deal with someone like that because you may find it quite difficult to reach them from any logical standpoint.

As an example of purported demon possession, Mark 5:1-20 tells about a man who wandered the countryside supposedly possessed by demons. Jesus cast out the demons and put them into a herd of pigs which ran off a cliff to their deaths.

Keep in mind that most people did not read and write in those times. They told stories and remembered them by oral tradition. The Gospel of Mark was not written down until years after Jesus' death. When people

Dealing With Religious Doctrines

repeat a story through oral tradition over the years, details may change.

Remember also that the Bible's authors wrote it long before the study of modern psychology. Aberrant behavior that seemed inexplicable 2000 years ago may now be explained by such illnesses as paranoia or schizophrenia.

I will share with you my simple understanding. You are a soul living in a body that belongs to you while you are here on earth. Your etheric body (soul) is a shadow of your physical body. It is your etheric body that makes contact with the spirit world, not your physical body. It is therefore impossible for another spirit, evil or otherwise, to physically take over your body. Those individuals who are very disturbed and act like they are possessed are really just mentally ill.

Pulling It Together

When and if you are ready, you will give yourself permission to explore ideas and practices that you have not looked at before. You will step forward with an earnest prayer in your heart and an open mind. You will know that the God of your understanding would never give you a gift without a way to use it as a blessing to yourself and others. You are ready to develop your psychic abilities.

Chapter Four

Psychic Development

Learning Styles

Researchers are studying the brain and how our physical, neurological, and hormonal makeup affects how we learn. There are different ways of understanding our learning process. We can look at gender learning styles, generational styles, cultural styles, and neurological styles. More importantly for our purposes, we can look at sensory learning styles.[16]

Traditionally, many of us have a preference in how we use our senses to learn.[17] There are:

- *Visual learners, who prefer to see or read something*

- *Auditory learners, who may retain more by listening*

- *Motion (kinesthetic) learners who need to perform the function to learn it.*

- *Combination learners who use more than one learning style. In fact, no one uses just one learning style exclusively.*

It is, therefore, very interesting that there are usually preferences in how a psychic receives their information from the environment. Most psychics will have a favorite psychic sense. Some will have more than one favorite. With training, you may learn to develop all of them.

The Human Mind

"Life does not consist mainly or even largely of facts and happenings. It consists mainly of the storm of thoughts that is forever flowing in one's head." — Mark Twain

Although we tend to think of ourselves as marvelous, unified beings, we are in fact a conglomeration of thoughts, feelings and ambiguity functioning in a massively complex human being. You may find that when you have a clearer understanding of yourself as a complex being, you will become more patient and self-forgiving in your learning process.

The brain is "an organ of soft nervous tissue contained in the skull of vertebrates, functioning as the coordinating centre of sensation and intellectual and nervous activity."[18]

According to popular culture, the left hand side of the human brain generates linear, logical and analytical thought. The right side of the brain produces creative thoughts, emotions, and intuition.

Yet from this amazing organ, the brain, flows the mind, with all its astonishing abilities and all its capacity to direct action. How we manage our mind is how we manage our life.

Meditation is a practice whereby an individual trains the mind to achieve an altered state of consciousness, either to realize some benefit or as an end in itself.

Brain scans have found that the brain activates the same portions by an imagined or remembered experience, as it does with the experience itself.[19] Therefore, meditation can activate or change your brain activity and affect your overall health.

Your brain produces different electromagnetic brain waves. The different brain wave frequencies associate with different levels of mental activity, such as meditation or other

Seeking Spirits

forms of relaxation like yoga. These states may produce spiritual growth or enlightenment.

There are many forms of meditation. A few examples are:

1. *Guided meditation, either using a pre-recorded script or listening to a leader*

2. *Focus on an object to alter your consciousness, such as a candle flame or an object you are visualizing in your mind. Hold the focus as long as you can.*

3. *Listen to mantras, chants, or quiet music.*

4. *Go for a long walk and allow your mind to drift into a meditative state.*

5. *Just sit in the silence.*

Mystics practise meditation in many religions, including Buddhism and Christianity. A particularly interesting collection of meditations are the *Yoga Sutras of Patanjali*. Sage Patanjali compiled them around 400 CE, taking materials about yoga from older traditions. They made a comeback in the 20th century. The Yoga Sutras are a condensation of two different traditions, *eight limb yoga* (Ashtanga yoga) and action yoga (Karma Yoga).[20] You can find books on the *Yoga Sutras of Patanjali* at Amazon or any similar bookseller. The

Psychic Development

Yoga Sutras have tremendous depth and can be followed for years if you wish.

These different forms of meditation can also be classified according to the sense on which they mainly focus. For example, if you prefer to focus visually to still your mind, you will enjoy a candle meditation or any other exercise that focuses on an object or even a chakra. We will discuss chakras later.

If your highest enjoyment is from sound, you will enjoy mantras, chants, sutras, or peaceful music. If you are a person for whom physical activity is most important, you may enjoy a walking meditation, yoga poses, or tai chi.

Eventually, you will want to change your preferred form of meditation to challenge yourself further. For example, if you have always been highly visual, change to an auditory meditation like mantras. There are many possibilities. Such changes will deepen and enhance your meditative focus.

In the end, it is not so important how you meditate. The most important thing is that you do meditate. Meditation is the foundation of many spiritual traditions.

Gautama Buddha, also known as Siddhartha Gautama, Shakyamuni Buddha, or simply Buddha, was a wise man whose teachings founded Buddhism.[21] He lived and taught in India in the fourth century BCE.[22]

Buddha wanted people to understand themselves better so they would suffer less. He learned by meditating and by observing other people.

The Monkey Mind is a term sometimes used by the Buddha to describe the easily- distracted, constantly-moving behavior of the human mind. The Buddha said that a person with uncontrolled craving "jumps from here to there like a monkey searching for fruit in the forest."[23]

In contrast to this, the Buddha asked his disciples to train themselves in order to develop "a mind like a forest deer." Deer always remain alert and aware no matter what they are doing.[24]

To overcome Monkey Mind, Buddha advised the practice of meditation. It will take time, but gradually you will grow past your limited mindset. The process cannot be hurried. The state of not hurrying is part of what spiritual growth is.

The Psychic Mind

Remember that psychic ability is one of the natural capacities of the human mind. Therefore, it makes sense to develop your mind to enhance your psychic ability. Most of us do not learn how to do this in school. Teachers encourage

Psychic Development

us to achieve a passing grade, often by memorization. The mind is capable of so much more. This is one of the reasons we meditate. It will improve our focus and improve the results of any psychic exercises we do. As we flex the strength of our mental muscle, the brain, we can teach it to hold the focus longer and longer. We begin to gain insights and feel calmer. We understand how we are really feeling and we are able to push extraneous thoughts into the background with discipline.

I find it interesting that some people have used drugs to enhance their psychic abilities. They seem to think it helps them tune in better. I would never recommend such a tactic – firstly because it is illegal! However, this reminds me of someone who thinks he is a great dancer when he is drinking. It may relax him a bit but he only thinks he has improved. Everyone else can see the truth.

I would instead recommend developing as much mental clarity as you can. Use puzzles, meditation exercises, and continuing education. The more you have in your mind, the more you can use as reference material when working psychically.

As for alcohol, I do not drink at all as I love mental clarity. Of course, this is your personal choice.

Seeking Spirits

The Psychic Senses

Extra-Sensory Perception (ESP):
The sixth sense is a sense beyond the normal five senses: sight, smell, hearing, taste, and touch. A person who has ESP will have awareness beyond these normal senses. The awareness can manifest in numerous ways.

Clairvoyance:
The term clairvoyance derives from the French words *clair* meaning clear and *voyance* meaning vision. It means getting visual impressions psychically about a person, object, event or location. A person who has this ability is a clairvoyant, which means *clear seeing*.

Clairaudience:
Clairaudience, which means *clear hearing*, is the ability to perceive sounds or words from outside sources in the spirit world. Psychics who are clairaudient hear voices, sounds, or music that are not audible to the normal ear. They receive these messages mentally or within their ears.

Clairsentience:
Clairsentience, which means *clear sensing*, is the ability to feel

the present, past or future physical and emotional states of others, without the use of the normal five senses. Sometimes we include clairgustance and clairolfactance in this definition.

Clairgustance:
This is *clear tasting*, the ability to taste a substance without putting anything in one's mouth. Those who possess this ability can taste due to sensations received from the spirit world.

Clairolfactance:
This means to smell a fragrance or odour of a substance that is not physical in nature. For example, you might smell cigarette smoke when you are in a place where it is certain no one is smoking or has smoked or the perfume that a deceased person would have worn when on the earth plane.

Claircognizance:
Claircognizance – also called *clear knowing* – is the ability for a person to acquire psychic knowledge without knowing how or why he or she knew it. The psychic can gain information about a person, object, place, or event through intrinsic knowledge. It just comes to the psychic's mind.

Seeking Spirits

Mediumship:

A medium is a type of psychic who can speak to the spirit world, that is, your loved ones who have died. Not all psychics are mediums. All mediums are psychic. I am a psychic medium myself. It is a topic very near to my heart. Teachers have written reams of books on mediumship. We will discuss it in Chapter 5.

Beginner's Development

I still remember those early days of my development when I sat in beginners' classes at various Spiritualist churches in Toronto. In March 2008, I found a dear lady who led old-fashioned psychic and mediumistic beginner circles in the East End. Her name was Reverend Bauld. She was half Scottish and half Irish, and more than tough enough to run a church of over a hundred people. Her mediumship was the work of a lifetime, and her trance work exceptional. The church was independent of others in the area, and the study material came from the United States.

Reverend Bauld was somewhere in her seventies, and her hair was still a beautiful flaming red. At the front of the church was a platform, and her collection of baby dolls were carefully arranged around the edge of the platform. Each doll wore a red wig. I will never forget the humor and the warmth of that circle. I will never forget the sense of excitement we raised when we sang. I learned much about how to approach this work of the soul. It was a terrific foundation for the training that followed.

I eventually settled into another church in the city for a time, and then found my further training at *Fellowships of the Spirit*. When I prepared to leave Toronto in late 2011, I made one last visit to the East End Church on a Sunday evening. The dear Reverend had been ill and did not see very well anymore. She remembered me and asked me to refresh the details. That was the last time I would ever see her as she died in 2013.

If I had anything to do over again, I wish I had spent more time in that circle. When you find a warm, happy, productive, learning environment, hang on to it for all it is worth. It is hard to replace.

Finding Good Teachers

Over time, I marveled at the skills of a few psychics or mediums and wondered how they managed to develop into such super beings – in my innocent view. The fact is, there are ways to acquire skills in most any area in life. This is the case with psychic abilities just as with anything else. You have a certain amount of ability naturally, but you can hone it. The trick is to find teachers who can help you unlock your potential. Then practise, practise, practise.

Of course, it is hard to find good teachers. It can even be impossible to find a suitable tutor within a reasonable commuting distance. You can travel far a few times a year or you can learn to do as much as possible on your own. One of the best ways to develop your psychic focus is to do concentration exercises. Concentration exercises build mental muscle and improve your overall focus in many areas of life. Properly practised, these exercises will improve your focus when driving, and when working. They can also make it easier for you to live in the moment, as you chase extraneous thoughts out of your head. More to the point, these exercises will help you focus longer and better when you are obtaining information through your psychic senses.

Concentration Exercises to Develop Clairvoyance

Exercise 1:
Sit quietly where no one will disturb you. Have a small handheld timer nearby so you will know the length of time you have concentrated. Start the timer. Close your eyes. In your

mind's eye, imagine a red ball. Still with your eyes closed, focus on seeing that ball in your mind. Keep focusing and try to do this for a full three minutes. Open your eyes and stop the timer. How did you do? Practice this every night.

When you are making good progress practicing with the red ball, learn to extend your concentration by changing the image. In your mind's eye, see the red ball and focus as long as you can. When you think you cannot do it any longer, without losing concentration, morph the image into a blue cube. I like to use pure primary colors in my mind as they are easier to see. Continue to focus using the blue cube. When you cannot bear the blue cube any longer, continue the focus, but morph it into a yellow pyramid. From there you can morph it into an orange ball, and keep going. You can choose your own shapes and colors. Simple ones are easier to focus on. See how far you can go with the exercise. You are building a new sort of muscle![25]

Exercise 2:
Sit quietly at night when no one will disturb you. Put a candle in front of you on a table and then light it. Make sure there is nothing else flammable close to it. Dim your electric lights. Gaze quietly at the candle and concentrate on it. Let your mind fly away to whatever images it does while you are

still candle gazing. It is helpful if you have a clock somewhere out of eye range so you will have a way of checking later how long you have sat. Eventually your focus will improve to as long as thirty minutes.

Concentration Exercises to Develop Clairaudience

Exercise 1:

Listen to some classical music. In your mind, pick out a musical note you like. Recreate the note in your mind, over and over. Repeat this exercise daily.

Exercise 2:

Find a quiet location where you can hear the sounds of nature. Relax into a meditative state. Listen to the sounds around you. Focus on them as you hear them. Try to do this for at least fifteen minutes each day until you find your clairaudience has improved.

Concentration Exercise to Improve Clairsentience

Have someone put a small object like a ring or stone in a plain, sealed envelope. Hold the envelope in your hands

Psychic Development

and pick up all the impressions you can through your hands. Check how you did and repeat the exercise occasionally over a period of weeks. You will find you are gradually becoming more adept at feeling the impressions through your hands. This practice is also known as psychometry (defined below.)

The Use of Tools

Tools are not necessary to develop psychically. However, they do provide a focal point to divert the conscious mind so that your subconscious, psychic gifts can be used and refined. For that reason, I recommend their use in the learning process. Always remember, however, that the gift is within you and is in relationship to the worlds around you. A tool has no psychic value by itself.

Tarot Cards:
Tarot cards were originally a type of playing card that came into fashion in the mid-15th century in Europe, especially Italy. They generally consist of 78 cards divided into the Major Arcana with 22 cards, and the Minor Arcana with 56 cards. Arcana is from the Latin word for *secret*. The Major Arcana is a set of distinctive cards, separately titled. The Minor Arcana is a combination of four suits, each suit comprised of cards numbered from one (or Ace) to ten, plus court cards: Page,

Knight, Queen and King. The Minor Arcana is the ancestor of today's playing cards, although the latter do not have the Knight.

There are literally thousands of different tarot decks available today, designed by different artists and reflecting their interpretation of the meanings of the cards. The imagery is often stunningly beautiful and serves as a powerful aid in interpretation of psychic meanings. However, I would not recommend Tarot as your first tool. It is too complex for beginners. Meanings exist on multiple levels and are best appreciated over time. I studied the Tarot for several years before I began to use it with the public.

Oracle Decks:

A simpler tool for the beginner to use is the Oracle Deck. Like Tarot decks, Oracle decks come in many beautiful versions. Generally, they are more basic and lend themselves easily to interpretation. If you would like to know the decks available to you, I suggest going to Amazon.com. Do a simple search and see what pleases you. A deck will have an abbreviated set of instructions. Start with a three-card spread: past, present and future. Do not attempt to interpret with your logical mind, but rather your psychic, intuitive abilities. Your first impression will be the right one. Do not overthink.

Psychic Development

Psychometry:

Psychometry is the ability to hold an object in the hands and determine information about its owner or events that happened around it. There are numerous types of items that are suitable for psychometry. An object that has been close to a person for a long time, such as a ring or pair of glasses, will carry enough information for a lengthy reading.

Flower Reading:

Flowers can be used in more than one way. You can start with a bouquet of flowers and each person in the circle takes one. Then the people in the circle take turns holding each other's flowers and getting impressions. The other way is to use them as a tool for mediumship readings. You take a person's flower and use it to pick up information from the spirit person who wants to make contact for that person. In other words, you use the tool according to your intention.

Ribbons:

You can use ribbons for a group of people who have paired off into partners. Use small, silk ribbons of various colors — samplers that you can buy from a fabric shop. Tell your partner to close their eyes. Choose a ribbon without letting your partner know the color. Pass it to your partner and let them tell you the impressions they are getting.[26]

Pendulum:

A pendulum is a weight on a string. It amplifies your own subconscious intuition, and works most easily with yes or no questions. It is an easy tool for beginners to use.

Crystal Ball:

A crystal ball is beautiful to look at, but can also be used for a type of divination called *scrying*. Scrying involves looking at a reflective object to see images, or answers to questions. . A crystal ball is not often used by beginners. Even if you do not use it, because it is crystal, it has a high vibration and can energize your work just by being near you.

Working With Others: Circle Work

Independent exercises are fine when you are just starting your psychic development. Once you have gained confidence, you may find it is helpful to connect with a group. If you cannot find a suitable Spiritualist church group, it is perfectly fine to set up your own gathering with your friends. This is a great way to broaden your practical experience. Be gentle with yourself and others and it should go well.

Psychic Development

How to Start and Run a Circle

1. Decide in advance what sort of circle you would like to run. You can have a circle for meditation, healing, or intuitive development. You can use it to share psychic messages or mediumistic ones. Define it as beginner level, intermediate, or advanced. It is not a good idea to attempt a general or multi-purpose circle, as it is then difficult to set and achieve goals.

2. Set your intention for the highest and best outcome for the participants.

3. Select participants with care. Try to find people who get along well with others, who are reliable, and who bring abilities to the group.

4. Determine time, frequency, and location.

5. Establish a suitable seating area. Ensure there is security or a locking door to avoid interruptions. Determine seating arrangements for the facilitator and attendees.

6. It is nice to establish an atmosphere prior to the beginning of each circle gathering. You can do this by playing soft music and lighting candles. Battery-operated candles are safest and recommended.

7. *Open and close in prayer.*

8. *If you are running a weekly circle, evaluate it after six weeks. Decide if the participants are blending properly. If they are not, try to address personality clashes and practical concerns. A group full of animosity is not a spirit-filled group. If you cannot resolve the problems, wind down the circle and start fresh.*

Chakras – Belief vs. Science

Subtle Body (Energy Body)

It is commonly understood that we are more than just physical bodies. We also have an energy body or etheric body. It is sometimes called the Subtle Body. According to the Bhagavad Gita, one of the most sacred texts of Hinduism, the subtle body contains mind, intelligence, and ego, which controls the gross physical body.[27]

Chakras

A chakra is an energy point or node in the Subtle Body.

Beliefs about the functions of chakras are thousands of years old. Like many belief systems, they seem to work only if you give them credence. In the 21st century, many people have cast aside mainline Western religions but are considerably less cynical about Eastern teachings. One might wonder if they are running to the East to escape the West. Nevertheless, it seems probable there is some basis to such a long-standing concept as chakras.

Currently a body of thought has developed surrounding such ideas as balancing the chakras, aligning the chakras, or cleansing the chakras. People talk about blocked chakras or about opening and closing chakras.

Recently, some people I know who regularly sit in séance received information from a wise being in the spirit world concerning the reality of chakras. Apparently "they are all quite present, correct and exist as the main areas where the power that animates the body flows inward." Then the wise being said "That is all you need to know." They do their job and we have no involvement with them.

Other scientifically aware individuals believe that chakras are whirling energy centers that exist as part of your energy body. They say that your chakras are open as long as you are alive. Therefore, you cannot open and close them, nor can anyone else.

According to scientists there are numerous types of energy such as kinetic, thermal, chemical, and several others.

Seeking Spirits

No one seems to know what type of energy comprises chakras. However, this is also true of other forms of energy we sense or otherwise encounter in spiritual pursuits. Perhaps the energy of chakras is of a form not yet understood, or one whereby sensitive individuals can perceive what exists in a separate dimension. With research, we may draw closer to an answer.

Research, experimentation and science may help us to a clearer understanding of the essence of spirituality itself. This is, after all, the 21st century.

However, it seems clear that the great psychics and mediums of the past in the Western world knew nothing about chakras and were able to function perfectly well. On that basis, I do not stress myself on the subject. Furthermore, I believe one should not take on board any more belief systems than necessary. A clear head makes for better reasoning.

Chakras do make useful focal points in the mind's eye for meditation. Many meditation CDs are available that guide you through the chakras. Whatever works for you, use it.

There are seven important chakras that line up with the spine. Interpretations vary, but from the top down, they are:

Psychic Development

Crown Chakra:

The crown chakra is the state of pure consciousness, within which there is neither object nor subject. It is violet and located either at the crown of the head, or above the crown of the head.

Third Eye Chakra:

The third eye chakra relates to psychic giftedness, and corresponds to the colors violet, indigo or deep blue, though it is traditionally described as white. It links to the pineal gland – roughly between your eyes and a bit above them.

Throat Chakra:

The throat chakra corresponds to pale blue or turquoise. It relates to communication and growth through expression.

Heart Chakra:

The heart chakra governs the colors green and pink. It symbolizes true and unconditional love.

Solar Plexus Chakra:

The solar plexus chakra symbolizes the color yellow, and relates to courage as well as vulnerability. It is near the navel.

Sacral Chakra:

This chakra is in the sacrum. It is orange and corresponds to energy, particularly sexual energy.

Root Chakra:

The root chakra symbolizes the color red. It is at the base of the spine. It relates to instinctive behavior and survival.

Auras

An aura is the purported energy field or energy body around a living person or animal. Psychics can often see the aura, whether spontaneously or with practice. They do not see auras objectively but subjectively – in their mind's eye. Then, they assign meanings to the colors, either with their own interpretation scheme or according to a system agreed by others.

There are also machines that assign aura colors according to vibrations. These machine interpretations may be different from what psychics say.

No actual scientific basis has been found for aura reading. It is another form of divination, done through means that we do not yet understand. This does not mean it lacks value.

Psychic Development

Color Theory

During clairvoyant readings, colors are often perceived. You will need to determine how to interpret them before you can share the information. You may choose to develop your own color dictionary or use the meanings determined by others.

It is helpful to remember that the colors you see are often literal rather than a symbol of anything. For example, if you see someone's Uncle Joe in the spirit world and he is wearing a scarlet red sweatshirt, it may not mean he had a red hot temper when he was living. It can mean his favorite color is red and he wore it quite often. Be careful not to over interpret what you see.

There are two ways to develop a color dictionary:

The first way is to write out a list of colors. Focus on them one at a time and determine what each color means to you. Set your intention to use the colors with these meanings when you are trying to understand psychic impressions.

The second way is to pay attention to your psychic impressions and see what colors stand out. For example, you may see a person wearing military green. How does this feel to you? You may realize that your own psyche associates military green with authority figures. This is the meaning of the color for you. Record such impressions and you will gradually develop your own dictionary of color meanings.

If you choose to use the color meanings that other people have determined, there is a resource widely used by classically-trained mediums. The meanings of the colors are accurately described in a small book titled *Color in Health and Disease*, a series of lectures by Dr. Hylton channeled through his medium, Irene Edouin, and published in 1937. A 2001 reprint is available online. It is important to remember that every book contains a cultural context and this one is no exception. If you are not comfortable with the Christian context of the book, realize when Dr. Hylton wrote it. You may safely ignore the context and take the information that makes sense to you.

Read the book through and absorb the meanings as they make sense to you. If you are working mediumistically, you will find the spirit world is intelligent and will work with you and your guides to use these newly acquired meanings.

Remember that color interpretation is like a language. It is an interpretation agreed between you and the spirits, and it is individual to you.

Psychic Development

Symbols

Every culture uses symbols. They are a wonderful way of organizing the ideas in your head. They can also be a very useful form of shorthand when you are dealing with psychic impressions quickly. As with color, do not over interpret any symbol you see. A good exercise is to sit quietly with a pen and paper and write down every symbol of which you are aware, like astrological symbols.

If you would like a printed resource, try *Signs, Symbols & Omens: An Illustrated Guide to Magical & Spiritual Symbolism*, Raymond Buckland, 2003.

When you have exhausted standard symbols, start to think of symbols that are unique for you. For example, when I see a Model T car, I think of my father because he drove one when I was quite young. Therefore, a Model T is one of my symbols for Daddy. You get the idea. Eventually you will have a powerful list of short cuts to interpret the information you are receiving.

Continued Development

One of the rewarding aspects of this work is that you never stop developing. There is always more to learn and there are new ways to experiment. There are many other tools that can be used in psychic work and divination.

Seeking Spirits

My friend was asked to work at a psychic fair for charity. One of the rules of the occasion was that tarot cards and other tools were not to be used. Being the amazing person he is, he found a way around the constraint. He brought a bowl of fruit. Each client would pick up a piece of fruit and hold it in their hand, focusing on their questions for the reading. Then my friend would psychometrize the piece of fruit, that is, pick up impressions from it. It worked quite well!

There is pleasure in continual growth and also in ongoing service to the Universe. The only limitations are the ones you set for yourself. Surround yourself with fresh ideas and look for opportunities to practise. Find ways to improve your focus. You will be surprised at what happens. The Way of the Mystic is a joyful one.

Chapter Five

TRUTH, MEDIUMSHIP AND SPIRITUAL DEVELOPMENT

SCIENCE AND PHILOSOPHY

In any spiritual study, a person is likely to encounter hard questions. One of the reasons for these questions is that everyone has their own opinions and ideas about religion and spirituality. It is a subject near to their hearts and touches on fears of death, misdeeds, and consequences. We have all been programmed by society in these matters and often the programming is not very positive.

One definition of truth is *anything proved by modern science*. Typically modern scientific methods, experimentation, and documentation back up these ideas. This is enough to convince most people. They will accept modern science that provides them with the safest and most efficient vehicle or the prettiest hair color.

Now change the conversation. Mention vaccines, newly developed drugs and GMO foods. This is a different discussion altogether, one that you will be fortunate to finish without raised voices. The fear level has gone up. They may not have the knowledge to assess these issues, and may accept pseudoscience instead. Of course there are points and counter-points for each issue, but you can see how easy it is to propel people into knee-jerk reactions.

I am not here to discuss modern pharmaceuticals versus other remedies or even other science. What I am saying is that truth is subjective. Your own experiences, the information you have heard most frequently, and your own fears and biases will influence your truth. It is easy to put up walls, and you may not even realize you are doing it.

Evidential Work

Scientific methods are put to good use in areas not generally considered to be science. We can evaluate intuitive work of various sorts according to the quality of the evidence and whether it is possible to obtain the information in some other manner. Scientists have evaluated many psychics and mediums this way over the years with various results.

The very finest psychics and mediums achieve roughly 80 percent accuracy in their work. However, a fraudulent person performing intuitive work would attain perhaps 20 percent accuracy at best, explainable as coincidence. Thus, accurate work proves something beyond what we normally consider as possible. It becomes another type of truth, yet no level of accuracy will convince a determined skeptic.

Science of Mind and the Law of Attraction

Other people have different views about what represents truth. They believe they affect an outcome with the power of their minds. There is some evidence that optimism does affect outcomes, whether it is by generating energy or changing our actions. I often tell my clients, "Pray like it all depends on God, and work like it all depends on you." Yes, positive thinking matters. However, I do not suggest ignoring scientific law and pretending everything is alright. If you need medical or other professional care, I would recommend that you get it.

Seeking Spirits

Spiritualism

Full disclosure here – I am a Spiritualist. I believe in the continuous existence of the human soul. I believe it is perfectly possible and appropriate to communicate with our loved ones who are no longer on the earth plane but live in another dimension, the Spirit World. Spiritualism is the only religion that clearly proclaims this. I publicly declare my beliefs and, like any true believer, I do not care much if others agree with me or not. I can tell you this path has changed my life and given me so much hope and joy. My life is never boring and the learning just keeps on coming.

Indeed, I have sought truth in my way, on my journey, for many years. I have entertained, researched, and practised a number of spiritual belief systems. There is truth in many of them. I am still a seeker, looking for further enlightenment. In this life on earth, we do not get an absolute or perfect understanding. That awaits in the spirit realm some time in the future.

Remember, I will never denigrate your path. Furthermore I am not here to proselytize you, to convert you to my faith. Why would I do that? You have free will. Mediumship, this amazing work, can also be practised while embracing a number of other faiths.

Even if you have no interest in Spiritualism, mediumship

is fascinating. In certain parts of the world, chiefly Europe, many people communicate with the Spirit World without becoming enmeshed in the doctrines of any religion. Why not explore what it is all about?

Little Children in Heaven

It was only a few months ago that Linda came to me for a reading. She was an elegant, composed woman several years older than me. She looked too young for a widow. She did not tell me her husband Steve had passed to the spirit world two years previously, but I soon sensed him keenly observing our session. He wanted to communicate to Linda.

This does not happen in every reading, but Steve wanted to tell Linda what it was like for him in heaven. "I have your husband here. He wants you to know he is in a very lovely place. He shows me a beautiful garden in heaven with purple flowers. He goes for long walks with his sister and his sister-in-law. They have lovely conversations. He likes to visit lots of other gardens there too. They are all beautiful." As I am a clairvoyant medium, I could see it all very clearly in my mind's eye. It was almost like a movie.

Linda confirmed that Steve's sister and sister-in-law were in the spirit world as well. It made sense that they would be visiting each other there.

"He was very happy to see his brother and some old friends again. His brother died a long time ago. Is this correct?" Linda confirmed that this was true.

"Now I am seeing a big group of children gathered together. There are more than I can count. They are meeting up with Steve, so happy to see him. He visits with them quite often. They look like poor children and lots of them are dark-skinned. One boy in particular is taller than the others and smiles broadly at Steve. Does this make sense to you?"

"Oh my," said Linda. "Yes I believe it does make sense. When we went through Steve's papers and his will, one thing surprised me. He donated a lot of money to The Children's Wish Foundation. I had no idea he was even interested in that charity."

The Children's Wish Foundation grants wishes to children who have high-risk illnesses, and whose families cannot afford special trips or adventures. If a child dies from their illness, they leave this earth with at least one wonderful memory. It makes sense the children would want to greet Steve, their benefactor.

I find it a great personal comfort to know that someday in heaven we will see the people we have helped. It is not a matter of getting something back for what we have done. It is just that the love we have given out freely will return to us abundantly. Heaven will be a beautiful place.

What is Mediumship?

Sometimes people do not understand what mediumship is. I like to tell them, "If I can read your mind, I am a psychic. If I can read your dead Uncle Fred's mind, I am a medium. He is in a whole other dimension. I am a channel or medium between this dimension and another one."

It really is that simple. Mediumship is not exactly like a conversation between us and the people who have passed over to the other side. It is more like a telepathic conversation. Therefore, if your Uncle Fred only spoke Italian, I can still understand him, even though I do not speak Italian. The conversation is from soul to soul. I can feel how Fred feels, and if he has messages of love, my mind is able to quickly interpret and communicate them to you in English.

I have always been a medium but did not understand that for many years. There is so much emotion and stigma around this wonderful gift. In our society, people are not comfortable with death. We cannot usually control when we die, nor can we control the circumstances of our passing. Death involves the loss of mastery of this life on earth. It is sometimes frightening even for those of us who firmly believe that life continues after death. We wonder if it will hurt, and what will happen to us during the process. We wonder what it will be like for us on the other side. One can imagine how terrifying the concept of death is to those people who have no belief or sense of eternity at all. Therefore, death is certainly not a topic for deep serious conversation. Furthermore, our minds are very efficient at shutting down ideas that other people find unacceptable. In order to fit in, we will subconsciously adjust our thought process. It is yet possible to rediscover actual truth even in our own self-concept.

The Purpose of Mediumship

Do you remember the first time someone close to you died? Can you remember how devastated you felt? How old were you? I was only ten years old when my grandmother died. She was incredibly dear to me and in fact served as my main parental figure. I had no idea how I would go on without her. It is amazing that I did go on and survive. The emotional damage ripped my soul apart.

Both my parents had emotional baggage and Grandpa was not a great communicator. When Grandma died, there was no one to talk to about how I felt. I became intensely shy and refused to smile for months. In fact, I never did get counseling or talk out my grief with anyone. It all stayed inside.

Truth, Mediumship and Spiritual Development

I was not consciously aware of everything I felt. It was largely repressed. I know now that such a devastating bereavement made me long for my Grandma. I am not quite here, so to speak. I have a foot in the land of the living, and a foot in the realm of the dead. Fortunately, I did not become suicidal. Somehow I stumbled through those years and became a productive member of society.

Of course, I was born a medium and at times felt Grandma Daisy near me, but I had no understanding of the gift or what it meant. I just thought I had strange ideas and emotions and did not dare to tell anyone. I already felt different from all my school friends. I was not close to any adult or any family member, and knew I would be laughed at and considered crazy. Things were already bad for me.

Now imagine how it is for someone who is not conscious of any spirit contact at all. Imagine the despair. You may have felt it yourself. There is no greater comfort than knowing your loved ones are still alive. The comfort is in the communication from them, and the understanding that the relationship still exists. Remember too, it means that you will not stop existing. You have a future on the other side of life!

Mediumship proves life after death is real. It helps us heal from our deep emotional loss. On the other side, our spirit loved ones can understand things they could not possibly know in the limitations of an earthly life. This allows them spiritual growth whether they come back to earth through reincarnation or not.

Furthermore, some forms of mediumship, such as inspirational, trance, and physical mediumship, can provide philosophy and deep wisdom from masters, guides, and other wise ones. The great hope is that our society will benefit from this shared understanding. What if we could find ways to move past war, injustice, and cruelty to a better existence here on earth? Would that not be worth everything we have suffered? In my view, this is the greatest potential of mediumship.

We are not responsible for those truths we do not know or understand. However, we do become accountable for what we learn that could better our lives on this planet. We may feel impelled to share our truth.

Who Can Be a Medium?

There are several views about who has the ability for mediumship. Some people believe it is a gift from birth. You either have it or you do not. A person with a modest gift can develop and refine it, but if you are not in the lucky set with good ability, you may as well give up and learn another hobby. This does seem rather snooty.

Truth, Mediumship and Spiritual Development

In my opinion, you must never tell an individual that they will never make a medium. For one thing, you could be wrong! I have heard unverified stories of students committing suicide when their hopes for success were cruelly shattered. Always be kind and allow hope for the vulnerable. It costs you nothing and can mean everything to them.

Another less snobbish view is that anyone can train for mediumship. All it takes is the appropriate amount of instruction. Encourage perseverance, and success will result. Many people will benefit from this approach. If it all becomes too much, some may lose interest without being terribly hurt.

Personally, I believe that everyone is different. Some have very structured minds and are most comfortable with highly organized work. It is difficult to persuade these people to try anything else. Certainly, there is no reason to push the matter.

Others can pull information from any source and in more than one way. They can be very successful. Many people are somewhere between these extremes. As in other fields, much depends on how much work and patience you put into the process.

There are some people who should not try to develop mediumship. These are the ones who are suffering from a diagnosed mental illness such as schizophrenia. Through no fault of their own, their mind does not deal with life in the same way as most other people. Some of them may indeed have mediumistic gifting but their health is of prime importance. Furthermore, when their mental adjustment is not good, any information received through a mental haze is unreliable.

Another caution concerns working with children and youth. When a young mind is forming and growing emotionally, mediumship development could possibly affect emotional stability. In my view, anyone under legal age – for example, nineteen in the Province of Ontario – should wait until they are an adult. There are exceptional young people who may be mature enough to proceed, but the teacher should obtain parental consent.

Our internal gifting and abilities will develop when the time is right. There is no need to push the process. The desire comes from within you. No one should pressure you. We all have our own pace of growth. Do not compare yourself to others.

Truth, Mediumship and Spiritual Development

Exercises to Develop Mediumship

Exercise 1:

This exercise requires a partner. Set up two facing chairs for you and your partner. If you have something on your mind that is bothering you, imagine setting it on top of a high shelf on the other side of the room. You can pick it up later. Relax your mind. Close your eyes and take a few deep breaths. Call out from your heart telepathically (not aloud) for someone from the spirit world to come join you with a message for your partner. You will feel a shift in energy as a spirit person steps forward. Do not worry, there are lots of spirit people waiting for the chance to communicate. Generally, this is all it takes and someone will step in.

Now that the energy has shifted, what do you feel? Are they saying anything? Can you see what they look like? Open your heart and mind as they give you some information. When you have three or four details about the spirit person, open your eyes and tell your partner what you have sensed. If the spirit has not told you what the relationship is (father, mother, brother, friend, etc.,) your partner may know. Hopefully, they will be able to recognize the spirit.

As a beginner, do not be hard on yourself. Just give what you get from the spirit to your partner who is the recipient of the message. You will have plenty of time to refine your techniques later. After ten minutes or when you have done all you can, switch roles with your partner.

Exercise 2:

You will need several people with you to do this exercise. Find a group of your friends or fellow students. Stand in front of the group of people. Close your eyes, take a deep breath and relax. As you stand there with your eyes closed, a spirit person will walk towards you. Get the easy details you can about them. Is it a man or woman? Old or young? What is their relationship to the person they have a message for? When you have these details, open your eyes. Tell the information you have received. Ask if anyone in the room can take the message. That is, do they know who the person is and if the message is for them? If no one can take it, go back to the spirit and ask for a little more information. Once you have determined who the spirit person came to see, you can ask the spirit if they have a message for the recipient.

This is the preferred method among some mediums as it gives priority to the spirit person that wants to communicate, rather than the recipient who wants a message. Again, patience is essential as you will get better with practice. Our time and effort are never wasted.

Truth, Mediumship and Spiritual Development

Exercise 3:

This is not an exercise for beginners, but there is no harm in attempting it anyway. Whether you are getting messages for one person as in Exercise 1, or a group of prospective recipients as in Exercise 2, you can use this technique.

Ask the spirit person for an object that was significant in their life, and that will help the recipient know who they are. The spirit will provide an item that is unique enough to serve as identification. Remember, the spirit world is intelligent. In a way, they are as alive as we are. The spirit will do their best to comply because they want to reach their loved one.

For example, in my life I often receive messages from other mediums in classroom and private sessions. In a private demonstration of mediumship, a medium told me a spirit was showing him a display frame. In it were lovely dead butterflies, carefully preserved for long-term viewing. This item saddened me and I was not keen to take it. Nevertheless, I remembered that one of my uncles had such an item. No one else I knew ever collected butterflies. I had no doubt he was the spirit person visiting. As a matter of interest, it was my atheist Uncle Bobby.

Seeking Spirits

Persistence is Key

You may find you can communicate with the spirit world quite easily. In that case, just keep practising to improve your work. However, some students of mediumship will find they need to keep experimenting with different techniques and teachers until they discover the method that works best for them. Every medium is different and will work differently. No one has the right to tell you to give up or that you will never make it. Approach this work with love, compassion, and persistence and the universe will reward you.

Mediumship Theory

Theory teaches us about what mediumship is. We learn in general terms how to do it. In other words, before you deliberately try to contact the spirit world, you should have some idea about what you are doing, why you are doing it, and how to deal with any concerns. In fact, mediumship is a huge field of endeavor. It is important to accept instruction and to stay as well-informed as you can. You will feel happier and less fearful and you will progress faster.

Practise

This is where the hard work comes in. For really good mediumship, you need to practise. Practise, practise, practise.

Truth, Mediumship and Spiritual Development

Do this for years. Find a decent teacher to evaluate you from time to time, then practise some more. Mediumship is the work of a lifetime. The good news is that it never gets boring.

You may wish to use the exercises I provided earlier, or you may wish to try other development exercises. Practise reading the public when you feel confident. Psychic fairs sometimes have openings for new readers to join them. You may find a local New Age shop or a Spiritualist church that will allow you to work.

The point of all this practice is to become better and better at tuning in to what the spirit world wishes to communicate to those on this side of life. The more you communicate, the clearer your channel to Spirit should become. That's it. It's all about them.

It is okay to charge if you need the money. However, it is best if you do this work simply because you love it and you have a passion for helping both the living and the spirit world.

Personal Spiritual Development

There are forms of personal and spiritual development that will help you attain better mediumship. Specifically, these include such practices as meditation, concentration exercises, and Sitting in the Power. Sitting in the Power is a practice whereby you regularly sit just to spend time with the power of your own soul. It will help sensitize you to the spirits who are around you.

One of the most important traits to have in spiritual work is persistence. Changes most often happen gradually and imperceptibly over time. The spirits observe us and act as our teachers. They will not give us more revelation until we show we are ready to handle it.

Fortunately, for true seekers, the spiritual quest never becomes boring. We will reach our desired goals. The only question is when.

The Christian Holy Bible says, "But the fruit of the Spirit is love, joy, peace, patience, kindness, goodness, faithfulness, gentleness, self-control; against such things there is no law." (Galatians 5:22-23, NASB)

"But now faith, hope, love, abide these three; but the greatest of these is love." (1 Corinthians 13:13, NASB)

Indeed, love is what will carry you through to the end. Love for family, friends, clients, and the spirit world will bring miracles. Love is the very energy of life itself.

Yet we never reach the end of growth. Once we reach a level of competence in mediumship — sometimes referred to as mental mediumship — more treasures of the soul await. Are you ready to hear about them?

Chapter Six

Advanced Forms of Mediumship

Spirit Inspiration

I love my Grandma Daisy dearly, and she has been in the spirit world a long time. When you are a strong medium, you tend to have a continuing relationship with your beloved family members. I have felt Daisy's presence near me many times over the years. She helps me in various ways. I have no doubt it was a joy to her to help me write the following story. Those lines about the hair standing up on the back of her neck and her heart pounding in her chest, made me feel like she was living it in real-time as I wrote it.

SEEKING SPIRITS

Daisy and The Bear

Let's take a little trip in time and space. We are in the small town of Oxford, Nova Scotia. Oxford is a farming community known as the Blueberry Capital of Canada because blueberries flourish easily there. The bushes grow all over the surrounding countryside.

It is late spring, 1901, and a little girl is walking toward us. She has big brown eyes like saucers, long straight brown hair, and very pale skin. She is short and skinny for her seven years and is wearing a play dress of bleached flour sacks stitched together. Her name is Daisy.

Daisy is going to the barn to feed some table scraps to the barn cats. She has a couple of bones for a stray dog she has named Wolf. That is great flattery for Wolf, because he is just a small, mangy black-and-tan shepherd cross. She gives it her best to put some meat on his bones, and has become very fond of him.

"Hi Wolf; Hi Kitties!" she says. She pets on the head all those that will come close. The animals are all a bit thin and devour everything offered. "Caw, caw," she mocks at the crows in the barnyard. Daisy loves all animals and avoids making friends with those destined for the dinner table.

Daisy does not love the black bears. Mommy warned

her that they are dangerous if you get in their way. They live in the woods near the farm.

Daisy works hard. When she is not in school, she helps her mom with chores and a new baby, little Flora. With six children and a husband who works long hours, Mommy needs all the help she can get.

Today Daisy is going to pick some blueberries so Mommy can make blueberry pie for supper. It is a surprise for Mommy, and Daddy will love such a treat! She puts her shoes on and picks up a small burlap bag.

The wild blueberry bushes grow all around the woods. Daisy ventures in and quickly finds and picks the first bush. She moves quietly along the path. She reaches the second one and something she sees out of the corner of her eye makes the hairs stand up on the back of her neck. There is a black bear on the trail in front of her, perhaps thirty feet away! He does not yet notice her, as he rubs his back on the bark of a tree to scratch it. She is lucky the wind is blowing in the other direction.

Her heart pounds so hard. Carefully she back away. Now he has seen her! As if curious, he moves towards her at a somewhat leisurely pace. Catching the scent of the berries he moves a little faster. Daisy can take it no longer! She screams, turns quickly and runs away down the path. As if encouraged to play, he starts to trot after her. There is no way she can outrun a bear, and he can climb better than she can. Panicked, running, tripping a bit she flees for home. Is he gaining on her?

She hears an outraged shriek from the bear and a ferocious growl from somewhere else. She dares to turn her head as she rounds a bend in the path. The bear has slowed, limping as he trots and she can see blood streaming from his fat leg. She sees a flash of black and brown fur – Wolf – disappearing through the forest. He has made a quick running attack and kept moving. The distracted bear hesitates. Daisy keeps running until she reaches a clearing near a road.

Daisy lost her burlap sack full of berries but suffered no harm except for a severe lecture from both parents. Wolf returned to the farmhouse later that evening. Remember that it honors Grandma Daisy to have a story written about her. She did not mind helping me.

It is my habit to ask telepathically for inspiration and guidance when I am doing creative writing or anything else that requires a little – or a lot – more than my normal abilities. I have many wonderful loved ones in Spirit, and many amazing spirit teachers who have stepped forward to help

Advanced Forms of Mediumship

me. Sometimes I know their identities and sometimes I do not. I am never totally alone, which is a great comfort in life. Why are they willing to help me? I think it is because my heart's dedication is to the spirit world, helping them to communicate with the world of the living.

You may say, how in the world do I know that? If you are a medium and work with the spirit world for some time, you become attuned to the energies of the spirit people you know. Every person, living or dead, has their own energy, or vibration. Everyone feels different. You just need to pay attention. You get to know your friends, so to speak. You may also receive messages from wisdom teachers who may identify themselves to you telepathically.

Spirit inspirers can help with bigger projects as well. There are types of mediumship that are not generally undertaken until a medium has developed considerable power and expertise in the field. There is no need for a medium to ever get bored. There are always new things to learn.

Inspirational Speaking and Writing

By definition, all mediumship is inspirational. That is, the medium performs it in a state of inspiration. Inspiration is an altered state by which you can connect to a consciousness beyond your own. The connection links you to your loved ones, or to other spirits who wish to help you with their knowledge, gifts, and compassion. They may give us thoughts, new ideas, or provide us with speaking material to share with others.

If you have ever been in an inspired state when writing or doing other creative work, you may understand already what I mean. It feels as if there is something outside your physical being that is near you and helping you. Thoughts may go through your mind that are quite unlike you, and are helpful in some way.

My personal belief is that, because intuition and creativity come from the same area of the brain, they appear somewhat similar. Many great creative people have acknowledged that it feels like the ideas are coming from outside their own minds. It is possible that creativity is a form of mediumship.

There are a number of sources from which we can obtain inspiration. Sometimes you will sense the source of the information. At other times you may not know, but the information is still valuable.

The sources of information include:[28]

> 1. *The spirit world — your loved ones, other evolved spirits, guides, helpers and divine intelligence or the Oneness.*

Advanced Forms of Mediumship

2. *Your soul — your own soul has its own wisdom which proves useful for much if you will only listen to what it is telling you.*

3. *Your subconscious or imagination — Your imagination is useful when you are seeking inspiration. Do not misrepresent where you get information.*

The types of inspiration can include various forms of writing, speaking, art, and music. One of the finest inspirational speakers was Emma Hardinge Britten, who did much of her public work under inspiration and toiled many years to advance the Spiritualist Movement. She published *Modern American Spiritualism* in 1870 and *Nineteenth Century Miracles* in 1884.

Do not underestimate the good that can come from inspiration. It is my belief that great wisdom comes not just from the logical faculty of the human mind, but also from the inspiration of the great, unseen powers of the spirit world.

Trance

Trance is an altered state of consciousness. The medium becomes passive with their eyes closed. Spirit intelligence will speak through the medium, often providing words of wisdom. There are various levels of trance that may be developed over time. Terminology is not consistent and you will often hear trance referred to as channeling. Channeling is another term that is not always consistently defined.

The trance exercises below require a partner.

Exercise 1: Light Trance Control:
Set up two chairs facing each other. Sit quietly with your eyes closed and go into a relaxed, slightly altered state. An experienced student will be able to do this within a few minutes. Your partner is sitting facing you. Telepathically ask the spirits to help you give the person a trance message. You are not looking at the person to read them or to find a spirit around them. You will find a spirit is somewhere above you or behind you. Allow them to speak through you with whatever messages they have for your partner. When it seems they have finished, return to your normal conscious state. Do not move too quickly afterward to avoid vertigo.

Exercise 2: Moderate Trance Control:
Again, you will sit in front of your partner and go into a relaxed, altered state of mind. Close your eyes. Telepathically ask for a spirit who wishes to address your partner to come forward. As you relax, you will feel a spirit come close to you. Allow them to come so close that you begin to feel their

Advanced Forms of Mediumship

feelings within your own body and psyche. Try to understand how they felt when on the earth plane, what they looked like, and how they behaved. You will feel the spirit overshadow you. Start talking to your partner and convey the information you are receiving.

Most often, your partner will recognize who it is that you are bringing forward. The very presence of the spirit comprises a message of love within itself. Ask the spirit if they have any specific message they want you to tell your partner. When you finish the communication, relax, thank the spirit, and come back into a fully conscious state. Again, do not move too quickly afterward.

Developing Deep Trance

Trance varies in its depth and takes time to develop. When a person is in deep trance, they will not usually be conscious of anything around them in the room. For this reason, it is not a good idea to try to do deep trance by yourself. In fact, it is not usually possible to do so. Deep trance requires more than just your own power and energy. You need sitters – other people who will sit with you and add their energy specifically to help you. Four people sitting in circle on a regular basis – perhaps weekly – will over time raise a powerful energy to help a trance medium to develop.

Seeking Spirits

If you are not so fortunate to find three other people to sit with you, even one other person is enough if you are both determined to produce the necessary results. Generally, the other sitters will want to develop their own trance abilities as well. Therefore, you will find yourselves taking turns to help each other.

Faithful practice will help you to attain deep trance. You may wish to record the sittings so you will know what information comes forth when you speak. You may eventually learn who your trance guides are. They often give wonderful words of wisdom for the entire trance circle or each of you individually.

Only about 20 percent of the population can attain deep trance. You will not know until you try. Perseverance is important. The spirit world will honor your self-discipline and they will help you progress to your capacity.

Physical Mediumship

Physical mediumship refers to the manipulation of energy and the manifestation of physical phenomena by mediums. Modern Spiritualism started in 1848 when three young women, the Fox Sisters, heard rappings in the walls of the home where they resided with their parents. Hysteria took over in their community, and the Fox family could

Advanced Forms of Mediumship

not rest for crowds of local citizenry waiting outside their home to hear about more phenomena. The sisters developed a code to understand the rappings. A spirit communicated through the rappings that he was a traveling peddler. It was later discovered that five years before the Foxes moved in, someone had murdered a peddler and buried him in the cellar walls. His skeleton was finally found in 1904.

Physical mediumship has occurred over at least the last several hundred years. It appears to have diminished since the heyday of Spiritualism but, contrary to the belief of some, it still exists today. I can attest to this as I have seen many demonstrations myself when I sat with some of the finest physical mediums in the world today. Physical mediumship did not stop in the 20th century. It only stopped being reported for a time. Today, it seems to be on the upswing again.

Spiritualists say that only a few mediums have the right energy to evolve into physical mediums. The process generally begins after trance mediumship has already been developed. Mediums continue to sit and eventually begin to produce phenomena such as direct voice, ectoplasm, and the movement of objects. The fact is, it generally takes a great deal of commitment, work, and time to develop trance or physical mediumship. Many people are not willing to work that hard.

It is true that some people will not have the right energy to develop into physical mediums no matter how hard they work. On the other hand, in rare instances strong physical mediumship seems to exist naturally. Everyone is different.

It is important to monitor conditions to ensure the integrity of the work is upheld. However, the wellbeing of the medium must always be of prime importance. Poorly controlled conditions have caused injuries to numerous mediums over the years. Anyone wishing to undertake physical mediumship should do a proper study of the physical standards necessary to protect the medium. Only invite sitters who are trustworthy and willing to lend energetic support to the medium.

It is easy to understand the need for mental mediumship (evidential mediumship as previously discussed.) Messages from the spirit world provide comfort to the living and the dead, and may help us evolve spiritually and find direction in life. The purpose of physical mediumship is not always understood or accepted.

The spirit world wants us to understand how powerful they are, and what they can do if they choose. The manifestations of Spirit can overpower the physical laws of this world.

Advanced Forms of Mediumship

These phenomena operate on the love vibration, the highest there is. The spirits bring love, peace, and good intentions. They manifest with their own voices so we will believe it is them. Many famous people from the distant and recent past have come through in séance with their own voices, with messages to help our evolvement.

I asked one of my favorite spirit people why this work is so important and why it must continue. He gave me images of a burned out shell of a plane in the forest – the desecration of war – and a sweet young deer – our lovely animal kingdom. If we could stop or even diminish the occurrence of war, and if we could improve the conditions animals endure on this planet, the spirit world would rejoice.

Remember we are part of the spirit world albeit still living. Earth is just our temporary home. We should want this sad yet ecstatically beautiful planet to evolve and rise in vibration. I believe we would all feel the joy.

Chapter Seven

HEALING

ALLOPATHIC OR ALTERNATIVE

Late May 2009 was a very special time in my life and I was having trouble containing my nerves. I was getting ready for graduation from a spiritual program that had changed my life.

It was Sunday afternoon. Some of the more magnificently crafted old buildings in Toronto were on display for public enjoyment. I decided to seek comfort in one of the stately churches with its fine display of stained glass and solid architecture. I gazed at the beauty and peace of the interior and remembered an elderly minister whom I knew had called the chapel home in the last years of his life. I missed him and wanted to remind myself of the Christian ideals I once held. I had been so sure I knew all the answers.

Soon, it was time to leave the cool dark sanctuary for the sunlight and hustle of the city. As I left, two ushers stood just outside on the steps to wish me a joyful afternoon. I smiled and shook first the hands of the gentleman on my left, then the gentleman on my right. As I stepped forward, the first stair step was lower than I expected! My right ankle twisted below me and I fell down hard with a smack! My ballerina flats were pretty but gave me no support whatsoever. There I sat on the hard cement step.

"Are you alright?" one man asked, and the other offered his arm to help me up. "I am fine," I answered proudly, and attempted to navigate the rest of the steps. Of course I am always fine and I stubbornly made my way down the steps and a block away to the subway.

I was not fine at all, and my ankle was terribly sore. In two days, I was traveling to Lily Dale, New York for my graduation week at *Fellowships of the Spirit*. I was destined for ordination as a Spiritualist minister.

My doctor's office accepts drop-ins,

Healing

and on Monday she saw me right away. My ankle was very badly sprained but not broken. She gave me a pressure bandage and a prescription for a strong anti-inflammatory that would reduce the pain and swelling. On Tuesday, I packed my bags and went to Lily Dale for graduation week. Then things got interesting.

I managed to take two or three of the anti-inflammatory pills. I rapidly developed a burning sensation in my stomach and bladder. It was incredibly frightening and very painful. A Canadian is safe in her own country with fully paid medical care. It is another matter to become ill in America. Did I need medical help?

It was clear to me that the pills were harming me more than helping me. I refused to continue them and threw them in the garbage. One of my fellow students said, "Hey, that's good medicine!" "Not to me it isn't!" I replied. What a horrible, painful experience. No doubt it was good medicine for those who could tolerate it, and expensive medicine for anyone without insurance. This was not a good start for graduation week.

Fellowships of the Spirit in Lily Dale, New York has offered training at *The School of Spiritual Healing and Prophecy* since 1988. We spent two years studying ministry, mediumship, and especially healing. We learned many alternative healing techniques. These are techniques not associated with allopathic – mainstream – medicine but other healing methods of varying provenance.

When one of the school's directors, Tom Cratsley, learned about my injury, he offered to perform a healing. Tom is a master healer with many years of study and experience. He is one of the many extraordinary people I have met since I began my spiritual studies. Tom performed a healing technique known as Energy Triangulation. If you would like to learn about it, you may contact him in Lily Dale, New York at (716) 595-3551.

During the healing, I felt the energy move through my body and felt considerably calmer. Within hours, the effects of the anti-inflammatory drug moderated. Over the next few days I would begin to recover, and eventually I healed fully.

As Tom worked, the entire class as well as mentors and teachers, sat in a circle to watch him. One of the mentors said to my mentor, "Ask her how she did it." My mentor turned to me and asked me what had happened to the ankle. "I fell on the steps of an Anglican church," I dead panned. The class broke out in laughter and for the first time I could see the irony myself. Spiritualists and Anglicans are well apart on the spiritual spectrum. Since that day, I have never tried to mix those two energies. I live according to my belief system and no one else's. I do believe it is possible to blend two or more paths, as long as you fully believe them.

I learned from this experience that allopathic or mainstream medicine is a mixed bag of good and bad results. Although it was wonderful to have a fine doctor with a quick prescription for my ankle, in the end, the remedy was worse than the problem. The alternative method had some benefits, and in the end my body's own healing capacities took over.

On the other hand, I feel one should never assume the natural remedy is the best one. There are many well-documented studies for allopathic medicine, and often none at all for natural remedies. Do not believe those who speak of documented studies but who do not produce them.

What is remarkable is that every one of the seven billion human beings on this planet is different. Our bodies may respond differently according to our own unique genetic makeup. You may find an alternative remedy that works better than other methods at hand.

I must caution you that nothing I write here should replace the advice of your doctor. There is a reason that health professionals need to study for so many years. Consult your doctor when necessary.

Seeking Spirits

Energy Healing

There are many options for natural healing that are outside the realm of doctor-assisted healing. Some of these healing modalities could be described as energy healing. These practices involve the transmission of energy through the practitioner's hands, either by direct contact, or by hovering near the patient. Some forms of healing can actually be transmitted over distance.

Such healing methods include Reiki, Qi Gong, Therapeutic Touch and others. In Christian churches, trained healers perform the laying on of hands. These forms of healing trace back to primitive rituals by medicine men and women in indigenous tribes.

The energy being given cannot be measured by electronic devices currently available. Therefore, it cannot be proved scientifically that these healing modalities work. Yet anecdotally, people feel better. Whether there is a real healing that we cannot measure, or a form of telepathy from the healer to the patient, or some other means of encouraging wellness, is not understood. Energy healing is a comfort to the chronically or terminally ill and many others and is therefore a worthwhile practice.

Healing

Spiritual Healing

Spiritual healing is the form of energy healing that is specifically taught in Spiritualist churches in various parts of the world. Healers have developed clear guidelines and techniques over the last 150 years.

Typically, the spiritual healer attunes to the healing guides in the spirit world. If the healing takes place in person, the healing guides will work through the hands of the spiritual healer. If the patient is in a distant location, the spirits will work directly and not use the physical hands of the healer.

The spiritual healer also attunes to the energies of their patient. With practice they will be able to channel different types of energy for different purposes. The guides will be able to use the energies for the most optimal vibration for each patient.

Not everyone believes in healing guides. Some people believe the healing can only come from the Great Spirit (God in all definitions.)

Much of the spiritual healing knowledge we have today came from Harry Edwards. Many Spiritualists think he was the finest spiritual healer of the 20th century. His methods are as valid today as when he pioneered them in the 1940's. He was also a physical medium, which helped him work at a higher level than most spiritual healers.

Seeking Spirits

I am proud to say I own a signed copy of one of his books, *Spirit Healing*, which was first published in 1960. He wrote seventeen books, mainly on spiritual healing. He gave forty years of healing to millions of people. He preferred to keep his methods as simple as possible.

Edgar Cayce

No discussion of healing would be complete without mentioning Edgar Cayce, known as the Sleeping Prophet (1877-1945.) Cayce was a psychic and medical clairvoyant. Daily he went into a deep trance state and channeled remedies for many thousands of patients. As every patient is biologically unique, Cayce's remedies for a particular medical issue would vary from one person to the next. It is worth remembering this when you are trying to get well. You may wish to review what Cayce recommended for your particular ailment. If one treatment does not work, try a different one.

You can find his channeled remedies in *The Edgar Cayce Handbook for Health Through Drugless Therapy*.[29] You can buy it from popular book resellers. A.R.E Press of Virginia Beach, VA has compiled this book from the *Circulating Files*, collections of verbatim Edgar Cayce readings and readings extracts.

Chapter Eight

GROWTH AND ENLIGHTENMENT

SPIRITUAL GROWTH

We have talked about meditation as a way to develop the ability to quiet the mind. In such a quiet, attuned state we are better able to listen to our intuitions and make spiritual connections. People talk about wanting to grow spiritually, and about using meditation as a means to that end. I have a question for you: What does spiritual growth mean, exactly?

I am asking you this question, because after all this is

your spiritual path here on this earth. If you are not sure what you are seeking, how will you know if you have found it?

It is the conundrum I faced early in my life. You cannot silence the mind or the heart for the sake of satisfying the views of others. It is the *Lonesome Valley*, in the words of Woody Guthrie.[30]

The more you try to force yourself into the mold of someone else's religion, the more your spirit rebels. You can follow the way of the Mystic, sometimes called the Seeker. As outlined in Chapter 2, Mysticism offers many alternative pathways and much spiritual freedom. Leave all the doors and windows open in your soul and see where you travel.

You know you are growing spiritually when you enter new territory and receive fresh ideas and questions that lead to more seeking. "Ask, and it will be given to you; seek, and you will find; knock, and it will be opened to you." (Matthew 7:7, NASB)

On the spiritual pathway you will have amazing adventures. I certainly have. I wrote about a few of them when I was studying at Fellowships. Here is one episode that is only a memory now.

Growth and Enlightenment

Astral Connections

It is almost 10:00 on a weeknight and my friends and I are in the online chat room of the spiritual message board we run. My friends are Bruce, a yogi musician residing in the Midwest, and Emma, a Norwegian-born housewife living in New Zealand. Missing tonight is Anna, an Italian-born day care operator living in Michigan, whose young charges are often with her long into the night. However, the three of us will have a wonderful thirty-minute meditation together.

"Hi, how are ya, love ya. Felt you with me today." This is our usual greeting. We feel a deep spiritual connection. Although we have not yet met or even spoken over the phone, our psychic gifts help us connect across the miles and in the astral plane during our meditations. Furthermore, we bonded powerfully the very first time we chatted – our third eyes connected to each other's heart chakras.

"Time." We quickly drift into a deep meditation. Our vision begins. We are in our usual green field in the astral plane, sitting on the ground yogi style, hands touching slightly. Although Anna is busy with her day care children, some part of her energy is with us. Bruce is across from me bathed in purple light. Emma is on my right swathed in angelic shades of pale yellow and powder blue. Anna is on my left, wrapped in muted shades of poppy red and dark green associated with her Dragon Totem. Bruce connects to my heart chakra. I am drifting deeper into a mist, away from our green field. The mist clears.

Bruce and I are standing near the edge of a grass-covered cliff, looking out over a large valley. I am a Native American woman, middle-aged and plump, with long swirling black hair. He is a medicine man, of Coyote Totem. I look at him and his head is not human, but instead is that of Coyote. Before me his head changes into the head of a hawk. Then the hawk spreads its wings and flies up into the sky and away. As it flies it turns into a Thunderbird. It alights in the Pacific Northwest as the Thunderbird in a totem pole. Then it transmutes into the ancient bird of Egypt, the Ibis – and the Ibis appears on an Egyptian hieroglyph.

Bruce and I are next together in an Egyptian temple. The temple is musty but warmly lit with candles. We are mirthful, having enjoyed a good party. Emma is with us, gazing into a deep blue stone and adding her power to the natural power of the stone. We are all Egyptian priests, and we are all male.

Then the scene changes before me and I see Bruce again. He is a runner between Native American tribes called Coyote Man. He brings a message to our tribe. I am again an Indian woman, this time in the Lenape (Delaware) tribe, Wolf Clan, in what is now the Northeastern U. S. I am living with the

Growth and Enlightenment

Lenape medicine man and his sister. He wears wolf skins and a wolf mask over his face. I have nowhere else to stay, as the white man who took me from the tribe has died, and no brave wants me. The medicine man is my friend Jack in this life, who is a shaman closely identified with Wolf totem. Jack even looks like a wolf. I share his Wolf Totem in this life, and Bruce has the Coyote Totem, which suits his playful, clever, freedom- loving nature.

Fantasy or Reality

What were these visions? Were they in some way past-life memories, or allegories, or only my imagination? Did they actually happen? Am I really past-life connected to my online friends, and did our intuitions bring us together once more, or am I making up reality by dreaming it, changing our past scripts? Much depends on one's concept of reality. The chills up and down my spine could make me wonder. I could see clairvoyantly and feel with my clairsentience the distinctive personalities of my friends.

I have no problem assuming the above adventure was totally within the imaginative realm of my mind. Even if this is the case, the dreams and visions have helped me prepare for greater wonders from the spirit world. There is no looking back, and my growth continues. I faithfully sit in the power and sit for Spirit nearly every night. I learn everything I can. The Law of Attraction tells you that like attracts like. The more time you spend on developing your inner self, the greater the rewards you will receive. "Energy follows energy."

We also know that what we sow we will reap. "Do not be deceived, God is not mocked; for whatever a man sows, this he will also reap." (Galatians 6:7, NASB) If you learn spiritual practices to help others, you will get a reward from the Universe according to your intention. This is also common sense.

Reincarnation

The human instinct that we are eternal influences the tenets of nearly all major religions and primitive folklore. We cannot imagine our own existence ending. Many people believe we come back in another physical form. Some believe we come back to work out our karma, the consequences of our deeds in past lives.

Reincarnation is a huge and serious subject beyond the scope of this discussion. Nevertheless, it is worth mentioning that progress continues in the spirit realm, not just on the earth plane. When we review our deeds from the greater awareness available in the spirit world, remorse and a wish

Growth and Enlightenment

to atone for hurtful actions is quite a common response. This may not always require an earthly body.

Instead, such a remorseful spirit will often look for a capable medium on the earth plane who can communicate to living loved ones about their new insights, changed attitudes, and continuing love. Such a message from the spirit world gives incredible healing, and can change the trajectory of a human life.

Enlightenment

Enlightenment is a Buddhist term for a fully evolved spiritual state where there is no longer any desire or suffering.[31] According to Buddhist belief, it is our final spiritual destiny once we have worked through all our karma or misdeeds and no longer have any need to come back to this earthly plane of existence.

Paramahansa Yogananda (1893-1952) was an Indian yogi and guru who introduced many Westerners to meditation. He is a rare soul who is enlightened according to popular belief.

When he died in 1952, it was believed he entered Mahasamadhi,[32] the act of consciously and intentionally leaving one's body. It is not the same as the physical death that occurs for an unenlightened person.

Now where does that leave the rest of us? As in other spiritual matters, enlightenment is a concept. Adopt it only if it makes sense for you. If it is true, you will certainly find out some day.

Meanwhile, we are all evolving spiritually, and it is impossible to judge ourselves. Perhaps we have many incarnations as we grow. Perhaps in a sense this is one long incarnation.

The Seventh Principle of Spiritualism is Eternal Progress Open to Every Soul. If we all evolve eternally, then does it not make sense that we will catch up with Yogananda at some point in infinity? Is he there waiting for us? Is time an illusion and it is all happening now, right this instant? You could always ask these questions in your next meditation. Record your answers. Then keep meditating. Eternal progress takes a long time.

Chapter Nine

CALL TO ACTION

We live in such an exciting era. Technology has made available to us much knowledge that our ancestors could never have. We can compare religions, ideologies, and dogmas without ever leaving our desk chair. Why not take advantage of the knowledge available to advance your understanding of Spirituality?

ACTION PLAN

1. Understand where you are now spiritually. Are you an atheist or agnostic? Are you committed to a religion or spiritual path? Would you like to

learn about alternative spirituality? If not, that is perfectly fine. Yet a conscious decision is better than ignoring the issue altogether. If you are this far in the book, I suspect you are ready to delve into these ideas further.

2. *I have provided you with a few suggestions for meditation techniques. Commit to trying one or more of them. Set aside at least five or ten minutes each day at a time when no one will interrupt you. A regular practice is more important than the length of meditation. It is not really necessary to go longer than twenty minutes to half an hour. Do not spend excessive amounts of time or it will be tempting to give up.*

3. *Start doing concentration exercises to improve your focus and thus strengthen your psychic and mediumistic skills.*

4. *Find a friend, friends, or Spiritualist church group to sit with regularly to improve your psychic and mediumistic work. Take turns reading each other.*

5. *Try some of the other techniques mentioned in this book.*

Call to Action

6. *Look for your next insight. This book has provided some ideas. It is your journey.*

7. *I am a highly experienced spiritualist medium and clairvoyant. I provide many types of guidance. If you wish to contact me for a spiritual reading, you can reach me at sheilajwatson@gmail.com. You can also visit my website at www.sheilawatson.com.*

I wish you the joy of your own path, the fullness of a life well lived, and the peace that passes all understanding. (Phillipians 4:7, NASB)

Resources

CANADA

The Spiritualist Church of Canada

184 Thrushwood Drive

Barrie, Ontario L4N 0Z1

(905) 691-7601

www.spiritualistchurchofcanada.com

UNITED STATES OF AMERICA

Fellowships of the Spirit

282 Dale Drive

P.O. Box 252

Lily Dale, NY 14752

(716) 595-2159

www.fellowshipsspirit.org

Lily Dale Assembly
5 Melrose Park
P.O. Box 248
Lily Dale, NY 14752
(716) 595-8721
www.lilydaleassembly.com

National Spiritualist Association of Churches
13 Cottage Row
P.O. Box 217
Lily Dale, NY 14752
(716) 595-2000
www.nsac.org

UNITED KINGDOM

The Arthur Findlay College of Psychic Science
Stansted Hall, Burton End
Stansted CM24 8UD, United Kingdom
Telephone: +44 1279 813636
www.arthurfindlaycollege.org

Bibliography & References

Blavatsky, Helena, *The Secret Doctrine: The Synthesis of Science, Religion, and Philosophy*. (London: The Theosophical Publishing Company, 1888).

Booree, C. George, "An Introduction to Buddhism." (Shippensburg, Pennsylvania: Shippensburg University, retrieved 10 September 2011).

Chodron, Thubten, *Taming the Monkey Mind*. (Torrence, California: Heian International Publishing Company, 1999).

Draves, William A., *How to Teach Adults*. (River Falls, Wisconsin: The Learning Resources Network, 2007).

Feuerstein, Georg, *Handboek voor Yoga (Dutch translation; English title "Textbook of Yoga")*. (Utrecht Netherlands: Ankh-Hermes, 1978).

Gellman, Jerome, "Mysticism", The Stanford Encylopedia of Philosophy (Summer 2011), Edward N. Zalta, ed. www.plato.stanford.edu.

Gregg, Susan, *The Complete Idiot's Guide to Short Meditations*. (New York: Penguin Group (USA) Inc., 2007).

King, Richard, *Orientalism and Religion: Post-Colonial Theory, India and "The Mystic East."* (New York: Routledge, 2002).

McMahan, David L., *The Making of Buddhist Modernism*. (New York: Oxford University Press, 2008).

Melton. Note "Chronology of the New Age Movement" (p. xxxv–xxxviii) in same work, starts with the formation of the Theosophical Society in 1875. (1990) (p. 458–461).

_ *New American Standard Bible*. (La Habra, CA: The Lockman Foundation, 1995).

Norman, K.R., "A Philological Approach to Buddhism" (PDF). *The Bukkyo Dendo Kyokai Lectures 1994*, School of Oriental and African Studies. (University of London, 1997).

Oliver, Paul, *Mysticism: A Guide for the Perplexed*. (London and New York: Continuium International Publishing Group, 2009) (p. 47-48).

Price, Patricia. *Psychic/Mediumship Certification Program*, "Part 1 Spiritual Unfoldment." (Lily Dale, New York: The Trilogy Institute, 2008).

Raju, P.T., *The Philosophical Traditions of India*. (Delhi: Motilal Banarsidass Publishers Private Limited, 1992).

Reilly, Harold J., *The Edgar Cayce Handbook for Healing Through Drugless Therapy*. (Virginia Beach: A.R.E. Press, 1975).

Tillet, Gregory John, Volume III: "Appendix 4: Membership of the Theosophical Society." (1986) (p. 942–947)

Twycross, Martin. *Course in Mediumship Study Programme*, also *Special Module on Healing, Inspiration and Trance* (DVDs). (Hampton, England: UK Academy of Mediumship, 2015).

White, David Gordon, *The Alchemical Body: Siddha Traditions in Medieval India*. (Chicago: University of Chicago Press, 1998).

Bibliography & References

Websites:

Bible Gateway: www.biblegateway.com.

Glossary Of Siddha Yoga Terminology, "Siddha Yoga Meditation." Siddhayoga.org. (Retrieved 25 July 2010-07-25).

"Guide to Buddhism A to Z," www.buddhisma2z.com.

Merriam-Webster Dictionary: www.merriam-webster.com.

The Oxford Dictionary: www.oxforddictionaries.com.

Vedabase: www.vedabase.com.

Wikipedia contributors, "Mysticism," Wikipedia, The Free Encyclopedia, https://en.wikipedia.org/w/index.php?title=Mysticism&oldid=723287501 (accessed 8 June 2016).

Suggested Reading

Signs, Symbols & Omens: An Illustrated Guide to Magical & Spiritual Symbolism. Raymond Buckland. Llewellyn Publications, 2003.

Colour in Health and Disease. Dr. Hylton Through His Medium Irene Edouin. Greater World Association, 1937.

The Complete Idiot's Guide to Short Meditations. Susan Gregg. Penguin Group (USA) Inc., 2007.

The Yoga Sutras of Patanjali (Sacred Teachings). Alistair Shearer Patanjali. Harmony, 2002.

Psychic/Mediumship Certification Program. Patricia Price, The Trilogy Institute, Lily Dale, NY.

Course in Mediumship Study Programme, also *Special Module on Healing, Inspiration and Trance.* Martin Twycross (DVDs). UK Academy of Mediumship. 2015.

Endnotes

(See the Bibliography for detailed information.)

Chapter 1:

1. "Again, the kingdom of heaven is like a merchant seeking fine pearls, and upon finding one pearl of great value, he went and sold all that he had and bought it." (Matthew 13:45-46, NASB)

Chapter 2:

2. *Oxford Dictionary*

3. Gellman, "Mysticism," Stanford Encylopedia of Philosophy.

4. King, *Orientalism and Religion*....

5. "Mysticism." Wikipedia.

6. Ibid.

7. Ibid.

8. Oliver, *Mysticism: A Guide for the Perplexed*.

9. Raju, *The Philosophical Traditions of India*.

10. White, *The Alchemical Body*....

11. Blavatsky, *The Secret Doctrine*....

12. Ibid.

13. Tillet, "Appendix 4: Membership of the Theosophical Society."

14. McMahan, *The Making of Buddhist Modernism*.

15. Melton. Note "Chronology of the New Age Movement" (p. xxxv–xxxviii) in same work, starts with the formation of the Theosophical Society in 1875. (1990) (p. 458–461).

Chapter 4:

16. Draves, *How to Teach Adults*.

17. Ibid.

18. *The Oxford Dictionary*.

19. Gregg, *The Complete Idiot's Guide to Short Meditations*.

20. Feuerstein, *Handboek voor Yoga*....

21. Booree, "An Introduction to Buddhism."

22. Norman, "A Philological Approach to Buddhism." *The Bukkyo Dendo Kyokai Lectures 1994*.

23. "Guide to Buddhism A to Z," www.buddhisma2z.com

24. Chodron, *Taming the Monkey Mind*.

25. Adapted from material from Patricia Price, *Psychic/Mediumship Certification Program*.

26. Ibid.

27. www.vedabase.com/en/bg/13/6-7

End Notes

Chapter 6:

28. Adapted from material from Martin Twycross, *Special Module on Healing, Inspiration and Trance*.

Chapter 7:

29. Reilly, *The Edgar Cayce Handbook for Healing Through Drugless Therapy*.

Chapter 8:

30. *Lonesome Valley*. An old American folk song recorded by Woody Guthrie (1963), the Statler Brothers, Elvis Presley, and others.

31. *Merriam-Webster Dictionary*.

32. *Glossary Of Siddha Yoga Terminology,* "Siddha Yoga Meditation." Siddhayoga.org.

www.ingramcontent.com/pod-product-compliance
Lightning Source LLC
Chambersburg PA
CBHW070628300426
44113CB00010B/1698